Praise For
You Want Me To Do What?

"Swamped with chores, why should caregivers add on writing? It gives perspective, restores sanity, releases stress, and deepens awareness. Writing saved my soul and brought meaning to my caregiving years. Writer, or no writer, journaling your way through this may help and inspire you."

Ann Davidson
Author of *Alzheimer's: A Love Story*

"Writing from the heart seems to be all that is needed."

Marilyn Ashlin
Educator and career coach

D1737343

"Any writer, experienced or otherwise, needs a place to start and a little encouragement. B. Lynn Goodwin offers this and more in *You Want Me to Do What? Journaling for Caregivers*, a journal keeper's guide by a woman who's been there, done all of it, and emerged with her sanity and sense of humor intact. Goodwin makes it simple and fun to 'put your judgments about your writing out on the patio, or send them out to play basketball, or buy them a plane ticket to Paris. Let them go.'"

Susan Bono
Owner of Tiny Lights, a Journal of Personal
Narrative
www.tiny-lights.com

Praise For
B. Lynn Goodwin's
Caregiver Workshops

"This workshop is an incredibly valuable way to get in touch with your own feelings and stop to take care of yourself."

Marion S. Wise
Social worker
New York, New York

"I am very grateful for the chance to say how this feels to people who will really get it."

Nancy Tune
Caregiver and writer
Palo Alto, California

"I can't tell you how many things I've sorted out by being able to write them down."

Diane P.
Former social worker and full-time caregiver
Santa Rosa, California

"Journaling helps; this sharing with others has helped even more."

Paul
Caregiver
Lafayette, California

"Writing each week was a very cathartic experience, and I felt relief afterwards."

JoAnn McGowan
Caregiver
Santa Clara, California

"I am especially touched by the incredible way Lynn has of responding to each of us. I feel passion and understanding in the responses she gives and have sat at my computer crying while I read them. They were happy, sad, and hopeful tears."

Eileen Reynolds
Caregiver and former office manager
Antioch, California

"It feels good to have an assigned space to put my feelings about myself and my mate...Sign up!"

Amy Halloran
Writer and caregiver
Upstate New York

you want me to do

This title is also available as a Tate Out Loud product. Visit www.tatepublishing.com for more information.

The opinions expressed by the author are not necessarily those of Tate Publishing, LLC.

Published by Tate Publishing & Enterprises, LLC
127 E. Trade Center Terrace | Mustang, Oklahoma 73064 USA
1.888.361.9473 | www.tatepublishing.com

Tate Publishing is committed to excellence in the publishing industry. The company reflects the philosophy established by the founders, based on Psalm 68:11,
"The Lord gave the word and great was the company of those who published it."

Cover design by Kandi Evans
Interior design by Lance Waldrop

Published in the United States of America

ISBN: 978-1-60696-297-8

1. Caregiving, Journal Writing

2. Self-Help Creativity
08.07.17

you want me to do

JOURNALING FOR CAREGIVERS

b. lynn goodwin

TATE PUBLISHING & *Enterprises*

for my mother

Acknowledgments

Many thanks to my Monday freewriting group: Kathy Briccetti, Veronica Chater, Annie Kassof, Suzanne LaFetra, Sybil Lockhart, and Rachel Sarah, who showed me, month after month, that these sentence starts were useful, open-ended prompts.

Special thanks to Joan Marie Wood whose freewriting workshop, Temescal Writers, helped unearth my voice and reignited my desire to share the power of writing with others.

Thanks also to Sharon Bray (Wellspringwriters. org) and Andy Couturier (TheOpening.org) for embracing the concept that caregivers need a place to express their feelings, hopes, and fears.

Thanks to the caregivers who are using these prompts and developing a journaling practice by sharing their writing through e-mail. I learn from each of their stories.

Thanks to Cindy Luck whose talk about a book

of prompts for writers triggered the idea to start sentences and let caregivers finish them.

Thanks to all the early readers for sharing their insights and encouragement.

Thanks to my family who taught me more than they ever imagined.

Table of Contents

Foreword

Journaling can heal a broken spirit. Writing can be your life support and sustain you through the difficult days as well as the sunny day. Journaling can be your vehicle to more sunny days. When you are feeling alone, journaling can relieve stress and lift your spirits.

The process of writing one's innermost thoughts is magical. B. Lynn Goodwin's book provides the sentence starts that begin this magical process of feeling better through writing. Her inspiring prompts encourage deep and meaningful writing. Journaling provides a safe haven to explore deeply emotional issues that continually swirl without landing. Her book is a place for swirling thoughts to rest.

B. Lynn Goodwin has a gentle and tender way of encouraging writing which makes it easy to start journaling. She offers an uncomplicated method of using sentence starts to write and process healing thoughts. Her suggestions for sentence starts are a helpful and inspiring method to work through deep emotional issues. Her book will help you to enjoy the process of journaling.

Marlene Cullen is a developmental editor, contributing editor to www.tiny-lights.com and founder of Writers Forum of Petaluma, CA. She has been published in More Bridges and Vintage Voices: A Toast to Life. For more information: www.thewritespot.us

… with writing you start where you are…You just do it—
you do it afraid. And something happens.

–Anne Lamott

Introduction

The months and years devoted to caregiving can be
vital, critical, limiting, and frustrating. They seem
endless while you are in them. *You Want Me to Do
What? Journaling for Caregivers* gives writing tips and
over 200 sentence starts to help hassled and harried
caregivers process their feelings.

Why?

James W. Pennebaker, Professor of Liberal Arts in
the Psychology Department at the University of Texas
at Austin, researched the effects of journaling and
found that putting thoughts and feelings on paper is
powerful. Journaling empowers the writer, who feels
heard and acknowledged. It opens up perspective and

insight. It reduces feelings of powerlessness. Research at other universities across the country confirms Pennebaker's findings. Journaling heals wounds and enhances mental stability.

I began journaling steadily during my first year of "Mom Care," a name I invented when my mother refused outside help. Journaling let me vent, process, and keep my mouth shut at critical moments from 1994 through August 8, 2001.

My mother was proud, beautiful, stubborn, witty, and fiercely independent. I loved her very much, but was often challenged trying to balance the roles of dutiful daughter and responsible adult. When we had no diagnosis other than aging and I could not reshape the world to meet her needs, journaling kept me moving forward. Later, it kept me sane.

You Want Me to Do What? is packed with understanding and motivation. It is an accessible, private place for any caregiver to work through the full range of emotions that fill a caregiver's life.

Use these prompts to ease the stress of caring for an aging parent, an ill spouse, or a child with special needs or a mental disability. Use them if you are in any kind of dependent relationship. They will help you process events, explore emotions, and rediscover yourself.

Why not give the gift of writing a try. It will strengthen your relationship with yourself and others.

If you do not record your own story, your tiny bit of the history of the human race is lost. Shakespeare wrote Shakespeare's vision. Dickinson wrote Dickinson's.

Who will write yours, if you do not?

—Pat Schneider, Writing Alone and With Others,
Oxford Press
Founder, Amherst Writers & Artists

Writing Saves Lives

As a caregiver, you spend every spare minute driving to medical appointments, stopping at the pharmacy, cooking, answering questions, paying bills, and helping with matters that used to be private.

Why write about it?

Writing gives perspective and restores sanity. Writing is a lifeline as well as a record. Writing saves lives. Do not underestimate its power.

One of the simplest, most private places to write is in a journal. It allows you to vent, delve into issues, and untangle messes. It lets you analyze or celebrate. It allows you to finish a thought without interruption. Journaling releases mental toxins and deepens awareness. It enables you to strip away the daily debris and let the strong, sane, safe, healthy, hopeful parts of you emerge.

What do you do if you have nothing to say? Look around the room for an image or a sensory detail—the way the sun makes a path on the carpet, the way steam rises off a cup of coffee carrying the aroma of morning with it. Listen to the high pitched whirring of an omnipresent machine, the tick of the kitchen's black-and-white kitty-cat clock. Tap into any sensory detail and see where the writing takes you.

Include sights, sounds, movements, smells, and the feel of the air. Don't worry if it's not related to the suggested topic, because topics are only starting points. Go wherever an image takes you. Explore fearlessly.

When you write in your journal, it can be all about you. The journal validates your right to be who you are and your worth as a caregiver. There is no wrong way to keep a journal. The only way you can be wrong is to refuse to write. Write anything.

Still stuck? Write, "Stuck, stuck, stuck," until something else comes out. Draw a picture. Keep the pen moving. You will get past this block.

Use the prompts in this book to ease the stress of caring for an aging parent or someone with Alzheimer's or dementia. Use them if you care for a cancer patient or someone with any debilitating, degenerative disease.

Use them if you care for someone with special needs or a mental illness.

Use them if you are a primary caregiver, spouse of a primary caregiver, or long-distance caregiver. This is the place to explore your frustrations and express your ideas without interruption.

Use these prompts if you are in any kind of dependent relationship. Use them to process the end of a relationship. They will help you understand what happened.

Writing is therapeutic. It saves lives. Get out of your own way and just do it. Your truths desperately want to come out. Let them spill onto the page and see what doors writing opens for you.

One of the few things I know about writing is this: spend it all, shoot it, play it, lose it, all, right away, every time. Do not hoard what seems good. Give it, give it all, give it now. Something more will arise for later, something better. These things fill from behind, from beneath, like well water.

—Annie Dillard

How to Write Your Story

Use the sentence starts in the upcoming chapters to begin your writing. You do not need to go in order. Start anywhere.

Write once a day if you can.

Not sure what you can say? Say anything. Here are three examples showing how different caregivers might respond to the sentence start "Today I feel…"

Today I feel poverty stricken. I hate having no income. The money you give me doesn't count. It feels like an unearned gift. I want to earn my own money, detached from you. I want to feel productive and independent. I don't want to feel like a nine-year-old doing chores for an allowance.

Selfish? Maybe, but when do I get to do what I want to do? Don't get me wrong. I love you. I know you need me, even when you toss your head and say, "I can do it myself." But when do I get to leave the stale odors and draining drivel of this place and do what I want to do?

Today I feel sad. You didn't want your breakfast. You didn't want to talk. Neither do I. I want to stare at the dust motes floating in the sunshine that's streaming through the screen door. So mindless. Like me. If I were a dust mote, I'd have no hands or feet or responsibilities.

Today I feel hopeful because Kristi is coming in while I go shopping and I'll have an extra hour. I've been e-mailing this really nice sixty-year-old divorced man on Craigslist, and today we're going to meet for coffee at Starbucks. I have a coffee date, and I feel like a teenager sneaking away to meet some hottie.

I know what's been in the news about Craigslist, but we're meeting in a public place. Afterwards I have to go grocery shopping, and he knows I'm expected home. What could go wrong?

How would you finish a sentence that started "Today I feel"? Try it right now, right here.

Today I feel...

_____

_____

_____

_____

_____

_____

_____

_____

Let the writing take you wherever it wants to. Feel free to make leaps. Trust yourself and trust the process. Write as much or as little as you want.

When you run out of lines, continue in your own notebook. Treat yourself to a beautiful journal if you like or write in a small spiral notebook that you can carry with you. Do whatever works for you.

Put your judgments about your writing out on the patio, or send them out to play basketball, or buy them a plane ticket to Paris. Let them go. They will be available to you later if you want them back.

Date the page—month, day, and year. It will matter later.

Here are ten writing tips to help you. If one of the guidelines doesn't work for you on a particular day, ignore it. Writing goes through phases.

Review these guidelines periodically if they help you stay focused.

1. Try to write for at least fifteen minutes at a time and try to write daily. That's a goal, not a mandate.
2. Start where you are. Start with the mood you are in. Start with what you see and hear. Start with what needs to spill out.
3. Write freely. Be specific. Lose control.
4. Don't think. Instead, let one idea lead to another. Dig deeply. Explore. Discover.
5. Respond only to the sentence starts that resonate

for you. Ignore the ones that don't. A response may come later.

6. Feelings ebb and flow like tides. Write what is true for you in the moment. When your truths change, write different things using the same sentence start.

7. Write about anything. You are not limited to the sentence starts in this book. A later chapter is devoted to your own unique sentence starts.

8. Write without stopping, or crossing out and restarting, if you can. From time to time, write a bit about the state of the world or the cost of gas and groceries. Look at a bad habit or explore your latest discovery. Write about specific thoughts, worries, and dreams. Write about the day you will be free from this phase of your life.

9. Go back and add more to any entry as new ideas pop up.

10. Send the editor that lives in your head on vacation. Maybe he'd like to join your judgments on that trip to Paris.

This journal is your personal record of your emotional truth. It is a place to heal and grow. Don't judge away your negative thoughts. They are only thoughts—not actions. Instead of banishing them, keep writing. As Julia Cameron, who came up with a journaling system called Morning Pages, says in *The Artist's Way*, "Pages are meant to be, simply, the act of moving the hand across the page and writing down *whatever* comes to mind. Nothing is too petty, too silly, too stupid, or too weird to be included."

Get your story, your nuances, your frustrations, your hopes, and your love on the page. Your story is buried treasure.

The fact is that blank pages inspire me with terror. What will I put on them? I suspect most writers are like this.

—Margaret Atwood

Getting Started

Still not certain which sentence start to pick or even which chapter to explore?

Start right here. Finish one of the sentences at the end of this chapter. Keep going. Go wherever the writing takes you.

If you can't write about how you feel, draw a picture: sketch a sunburst, a storm cloud, a fist, or a rainbow. Put yourself on a riverbank with a fishing pole or behind a CEO's desk or on a Caribbean cruise. Trust yourself and let your thoughts go wherever they want. Reuse these starting lines as often as you like.

Let the sentence starts below help you discover whether you want to write about yourself, the one you take care of, the art of caregiving, or reclaiming yourself today.

Today I feel…

_____

_____

_____

_____

_____

_____

Today I believe…

_____

_____

_____

_____

_____

_____

Today I want…

_____

_____

_____

_____

_____

_____

Today I am…

_____

_____

_____

_____

_____

Today I hope…

_____

_____

_____

_____

_____

_____

In the middle of the world, make one positive step. In the center of chaos, make one definitive act. Just write.

—Natalie Goldberg

Thoughts about Me

Imagine you are on an airplane, and the oxygen mask drops in front of you. You need to put on your own mask before attending to the needs of anyone else, right? This chapter encourages you to take care of yourself in exactly the same way. Make some time to nurture yourself, and you will have more to give the others in your life.

The truth is…

_____
_____
_____
_____
_____
_____
_____
_____
_____

Yesterday, I believed…

_____
_____
_____
_____
_____
_____
_____
_____
_____

I am…

_____

_____

_____

_____

_____

_____

_____

_____

Today, I know…

_____

_____

_____

_____

_____

_____

_____

_____

Today, I want…

_____

_____

_____

_____

_____

_____

_____

_____

I used to be…

_____

_____

_____

_____

_____

_____

_____

_____

Today, I don't want...

_____

_____

_____

_____

_____

_____

_____

_____

Inside of me...

_____

_____

_____

_____

_____

_____

_____

_____

I tried…

_____

_____

_____

_____

_____

_____

_____

_____

Sometimes I wonder…

_____

_____

_____

_____

_____

_____

_____

_____

No one knows I worry about…

_____

_____

_____

_____

_____

_____

_____

_____

_____

The last time I talked to my best friend…

_____

_____

_____

_____

_____

_____

_____

_____

_____

I have great respect for…

_____

_____

_____

_____

_____

_____

_____

_____

I don't like to brag, but…

_____

_____

_____

_____

_____

_____

_____

_____

When my children need me...

_____
_____
_____
_____
_____
_____
_____
_____

When my partner wants attention...

_____
_____
_____
_____
_____
_____
_____
_____

I am still reluctant to…

_____

_____

_____

_____

_____

_____

_____

_____

I no longer understand…

_____

_____

_____

_____

_____

_____

_____

_____

B. LYNN GOODWIN

If I were in charge…

_____

_____

_____

_____

_____

_____

_____

_____

I love the smell of…

_____

_____

_____

_____

_____

_____

_____

I'm always thinking...

_____

_____

_____

_____

_____

_____

_____

_____

I can barely remember...

_____

_____

_____

_____

_____

_____

_____

_____

If I ever talk in my sleep…

_____

_____

_____

_____

_____

_____

_____

_____

It has always been fun to…

_____

_____

_____

_____

_____

_____

_____

_____

Because I followed…

_____
_____
_____
_____
_____
_____
_____
_____

I usually don't talk about…

_____
_____
_____
_____
_____
_____
_____
_____

B. LYNN GOODWIN

If I let myself cry…

_____

_____

_____

_____

_____

_____

_____

_____

Secrets make me…

_____

_____

_____

_____

_____

_____

_____

I was so proud…

_____

_____

_____

_____

_____

_____

_____

_____

I remember…

_____

_____

_____

_____

_____

_____

_____

_____

I don't remember…

_____

_____

_____

_____

_____

_____

_____

_____

I wish I could remember…

_____

_____

_____

_____

_____

_____

_____

_____

Today, I clearly recall…

_____

_____

_____

_____

_____

_____

_____

_____

A year ago…

_____

_____

_____

_____

_____

_____

_____

_____

B. LYNN GOODWIN

Five years ago…

_____
_____
_____
_____
_____
_____
_____
_____

Ten years ago…

_____
_____
_____
_____
_____
_____
_____
_____

In the room where I grew up…

_____

_____

_____

_____

_____

_____

_____

_____

I wonder…

_____

_____

_____

_____

_____

_____

_____

I lost faith when…

_____

_____

_____

_____

_____

_____

_____

_____

I no longer know…

_____

_____

_____

_____

_____

_____

_____

_____

I lust after…

_____

_____

_____

_____

_____

_____

_____

_____

I gained faith when…

_____

_____

_____

_____

_____

_____

_____

_____

B. LYNN GOODWIN

Today my best moments are...

_____
_____
_____
_____
_____
_____
_____
_____

I get so frustrated when...

_____
_____
_____
_____
_____
_____
_____

I didn't always think…

_____

_____

_____

_____

_____

_____

_____

_____

Hope…

_____

_____

_____

_____

_____

_____

_____

_____

B. LYNN GOODWIN

My face went red and my skin grew hot when…

_____

_____

_____

_____

_____

_____

_____

_____

_____

Optimism…

_____

_____

_____

_____

_____

_____

_____

_____

I wish I didn't resent…

_____

_____

_____

_____

_____

_____

_____

_____

I'm teetering on…

_____

_____

_____

_____

_____

_____

_____

_____

This morning…

_____

_____

_____

_____

_____

_____

_____

_____

_____

Next time…

_____

_____

_____

_____

_____

_____

_____

_____

_____

Peace has become…

_____

_____

_____

_____

_____

_____

_____

_____

I love…

_____

_____

_____

_____

_____

_____

_____

_____

B. LYNN GOODWIN

It is easy to love people in memory; the hard trick is to love them when they are there, in front of you.

—John Updike

Thoughts about Caregiving

In this chapter, the focus shifts to caregiving. Which parts give you joy? Which parts do you resent? What do you miss about your old life, and what do you love about your new life?

If you ask me…

_____

_____

_____

_____

_____

_____

_____

_____

When I want to escape…

_____

_____

_____

_____

_____

_____

_____

_____

When I came into your room this morning...

_____

_____

_____

_____

_____

_____

_____

_____

It's hard to admit...

_____

_____

_____

_____

_____

_____

_____

_____

Following…

_____

_____

_____

_____

_____

_____

_____

_____

Our best day…

_____

_____

_____

_____

_____

_____

_____

B. LYNN GOODWIN

When we go out...

_____

_____

_____

_____

_____

_____

_____

_____

Today I will focus on...

_____

_____

_____

_____

_____

_____

_____

_____

Whenever I open the door to your place...

_____

_____

_____

_____

_____

_____

_____

_____

We don't need...

_____

_____

_____

_____

_____

_____

_____

_____

B. LYNN GOODWIN

Because…

_____

_____

_____

_____

_____

_____

_____

_____

Our truth is…

_____

_____

_____

_____

_____

_____

_____

_____

My life changed forever when…

_____

_____

_____

_____

_____

_____

_____

_____

After I hung up the phone…

_____

_____

_____

_____

_____

_____

_____

_____

Someone else might have walked away when...

_____

_____

_____

_____

_____

_____

_____

_____

_____

Doctors and nurses...

_____

_____

_____

_____

_____

_____

_____

_____

_____

What if…

_____
_____
_____
_____
_____
_____
_____
_____

Everything that matters takes…

_____
_____
_____
_____
_____
_____
_____
_____

B. LYNN GOODWIN

Although it was risky…

_____

_____

_____

_____

_____

_____

_____

_____

Before you wake up…

_____

_____

_____

_____

_____

_____

_____

_____

Loneliness…

_____

_____

_____

_____

_____

_____

_____

_____

At sunset…

_____

_____

_____

_____

_____

_____

_____

_____

B . L Y N N G O O D W I N

Chocolate always…

_____

_____

_____

_____

_____

_____

_____

_____

Meals used to be…

_____

_____

_____

_____

_____

_____

_____

_____

The kitchen smelled sharply of...

_____

_____

_____

_____

_____

_____

_____

_____

Day after day...

_____

_____

_____

_____

_____

_____

_____

_____

B. LYNN GOODWIN

I was thrilled when…

_____

_____

_____

_____

_____

_____

_____

_____

I feel isolated when…

_____

_____

_____

_____

_____

_____

_____

_____

Sometimes I'm scared to death that…

_____

_____

_____

_____

_____

_____

_____

_____

No one thinks…

_____

_____

_____

_____

_____

_____

_____

_____

B. LYNN GOODWIN

I froze when…

_____

_____

_____

_____

_____

_____

_____

_____

In the darkened apartment…

_____

_____

_____

_____

_____

_____

_____

_____

Stress is…

_____
_____
_____
_____
_____
_____
_____
_____

The steady murmur of traffic on the interstate…

_____
_____
_____
_____
_____
_____
_____
_____

If I could change one thing in our routine...

_____
_____
_____
_____
_____
_____
_____
_____

I have become a haunter of...

_____
_____
_____
_____
_____
_____
_____
_____

Across the street...

_____
_____
_____
_____
_____
_____
_____
_____

In other countries...

_____
_____
_____
_____
_____
_____
_____
_____

B. LYNN GOODWIN

When…

_____
_____
_____
_____
_____
_____
_____
_____
_____

Regularly…

_____
_____
_____
_____
_____
_____
_____
_____
_____

You forget how it feels to…

_____

_____

_____

_____

_____

_____

_____

_____

I wish I could trust you to…

_____

_____

_____

_____

_____

_____

_____

_____

I feel burned out when…

_____
_____
_____
_____
_____
_____
_____
_____

Relentlessly…

_____
_____
_____
_____
_____
_____
_____
_____

A deep breath…

_____

_____

_____

_____

_____

_____

_____

_____

If need be…

_____

_____

_____

_____

_____

_____

_____

_____

B . L Y N N G O O D W I N

I hate it when people treat you...

_____

_____

_____

_____

_____

_____

_____

_____

_____

When do I get to...

_____

_____

_____

_____

_____

_____

_____

_____

When someone tells you to…

_____
_____
_____
_____
_____
_____
_____
_____
_____

I wish more people cared about…

_____
_____
_____
_____
_____
_____
_____
_____

It's still fun to…

_____

_____

_____

_____

_____

_____

_____

_____

_____

I've never told you…

_____

_____

_____

_____

_____

_____

_____

_____

Despite everything, I'm still…

_____

_____

_____

_____

_____

_____

_____

_____

_____

B. LYNN GOODWIN

Writing is like touching old scar tissue.

—Anonymous

Thoughts about the One I Care For

Look at your relationship and how it has evolved. What did it used to be like? How have your roles changed? What are your best, worst, and strongest memories? Why do you care?

I've heard that you began life as…

_____

_____

_____

_____

_____

_____

_____

_____

_____

Remember when you told me…

_____

_____

_____

_____

_____

_____

_____

_____

Today you are…

_____

_____

_____

_____

_____

_____

_____

_____

I am grateful…

_____

_____

_____

_____

_____

_____

_____

Twenty years ago…

_____

_____

_____

_____

_____

_____

_____

_____

At the edge of my heart…

_____

_____

_____

_____

_____

_____

_____

_____

Do you recall…

_____

_____

_____

_____

_____

_____

_____

_____

Today you want…

_____

_____

_____

_____

_____

_____

_____

_____

You control...

_____

_____

_____

_____

_____

_____

_____

_____

I am grateful I never told you that...

_____

_____

_____

_____

_____

_____

_____

_____

B. LYNN GOODWIN

When I touch you…

_____
_____
_____
_____
_____
_____
_____
_____

Our best holiday…

_____
_____
_____
_____
_____
_____
_____
_____

I wish you could still remember…

_____

_____

_____

_____

_____

_____

_____

_____

You always said…

_____

_____

_____

_____

_____

_____

_____

_____

B. LYNN GOODWIN

You used to be…

_____

_____

_____

_____

_____

_____

_____

_____

I love you, and…

_____

_____

_____

_____

_____

_____

_____

_____

I love you, but…

_____

_____

_____

_____

_____

_____

_____

_____

Despite your condition…

_____

_____

_____

_____

_____

_____

_____

You never seem to…

_____

_____

_____

_____

_____

_____

_____

_____

Our decision…

_____

_____

_____

_____

_____

_____

_____

_____

Have you noticed…

_____

_____

_____

_____

_____

_____

_____

Do you still believe…

_____

_____

_____

_____

_____

_____

_____

B. LYNN GOODWIN

What are we going to do about…

_____

_____

_____

_____

_____

_____

_____

_____

I'm glad you no longer remember…

_____

_____

_____

_____

_____

_____

_____

_____

I have trouble telling you...

_____

_____

_____

_____

_____

_____

_____

_____

When we were both younger...

_____

_____

_____

_____

_____

_____

_____

_____

B . L Y N N G O O D W I N

You used to need…

_____

_____

_____

_____

_____

_____

_____

_____

Today you need…

_____

_____

_____

_____

_____

_____

_____

_____

After…

_____

_____

_____

_____

_____

_____

_____

_____

In this photo…

_____

_____

_____

_____

_____

_____

_____

When I opened the envelope…

_____
_____
_____
_____
_____
_____
_____
_____

Have you ever wondered…

_____
_____
_____
_____
_____
_____
_____
_____

I'm afraid to ask you...

_____

_____

_____

_____

_____

_____

_____

_____

If I were you...

_____

_____

_____

_____

_____

_____

_____

_____

B. LYNN GOODWIN

I wish you knew…

_____
_____
_____
_____
_____
_____
_____
_____
_____

You told me…

_____
_____
_____
_____
_____
_____
_____
_____
_____

The fear in your eyes…

_____

_____

_____

_____

_____

_____

_____

_____

Do you ever think about…

_____

_____

_____

_____

_____

_____

_____

_____

B. LYNN GOODWIN

My life is easier because you don't know...

_____

_____

_____

_____

_____

_____

_____

_____

Today you know...

_____

_____

_____

_____

_____

_____

_____

_____

So many questions rose up when…

_____

_____

_____

_____

_____

_____

_____

_____

Smoldering…

_____

_____

_____

_____

_____

_____

_____

_____

You no longer need…

_____

_____

_____

_____

_____

_____

_____

_____

_____

Because of the things I said…

_____

_____

_____

_____

_____

_____

_____

_____

I wish I understood…

_____

_____

_____

_____

_____

_____

_____

_____

How much longer will you…

_____

_____

_____

_____

_____

_____

_____

_____

B . L Y N N G O O D W I N

If only…

_____

_____

_____

_____

_____

_____

_____

_____

Because of you…

_____

_____

_____

_____

_____

_____

_____

_____

Your laughter makes me…

_____

_____

_____

_____

_____

_____

_____

_____

When I open my heart…

_____

_____

_____

_____

_____

_____

_____

_____

Everybody is talented, original, and has something important to say.

—Barbara Ueland

Thoughts about Reclaiming Myself

We've come full circle. Let the optimistic flavor of these sentence starts transport you to the world you will someday inhabit.

When I let go I will discover…

_____

_____

_____

_____

_____

_____

_____

_____

It will be fun to…

_____

_____

_____

_____

_____

_____

_____

_____

If I were my own guardian angel…

_____

_____

_____

_____

_____

_____

_____

_____

Recovering from…

_____

_____

_____

_____

_____

_____

_____

_____

When I listen to…

_____
_____
_____
_____
_____
_____
_____
_____
_____

I promise myself…

_____
_____
_____
_____
_____
_____
_____
_____

B . L Y N N   G O O D W I N

From my kitchen window...

_____
_____
_____
_____
_____
_____
_____
_____

Fate...

_____
_____
_____
_____
_____
_____
_____
_____

Escape…

_____
_____
_____
_____
_____
_____
_____
_____

I am no longer in such a hurry to…

_____
_____
_____
_____
_____
_____
_____

B. LYNN GOODWIN

Although I used to believe…

_____

_____

_____

_____

_____

_____

_____

What if…

_____

_____

_____

_____

_____

_____

_____

_____

My healing…

_____

_____

_____

_____

_____

_____

_____

_____

Success now means…

_____

_____

_____

_____

_____

_____

_____

_____

I hope…

_____

_____

_____

_____

_____

_____

_____

_____

The eyes in the mirror…

_____

_____

_____

_____

_____

_____

_____

_____

Parents and children should…

_____
_____
_____
_____
_____
_____
_____
_____
_____

Today I will focus on…

_____
_____
_____
_____
_____
_____
_____
_____
_____

B. LYNN GOODWIN

Anticipating…

_____

_____

_____

_____

_____

_____

_____

_____

Acceptance has become…

_____

_____

_____

_____

_____

_____

_____

_____

The scent of…

_____

_____

_____

_____

_____

_____

_____

_____

I am ready to explore…

_____

_____

_____

_____

_____

_____

_____

B. LYNN GOODWIN

Forgiveness comes to…

_____

_____

_____

_____

_____

_____

_____

_____

In my wildest dreams…

_____

_____

_____

_____

_____

_____

_____

_____

When I met a new...

_____

_____

_____

_____

_____

_____

_____

_____

The other day...

_____

_____

_____

_____

_____

_____

_____

_____

I forget what it feels like to…

_____
_____
_____
_____
_____
_____
_____
_____

Running from…

_____
_____
_____
_____
_____
_____
_____
_____

Taking deep breaths…

_____

_____

_____

_____

_____

_____

_____

_____

If I listen to…

_____

_____

_____

_____

_____

_____

_____

_____

Some years ago I…

_____
_____
_____
_____
_____
_____
_____
_____

When I exercise…

_____
_____
_____
_____
_____
_____
_____
_____

If someone asked me...

_____
_____
_____
_____
_____
_____
_____
_____

Out on the freeway...

_____
_____
_____
_____
_____
_____
_____
_____

B. LYNN GOODWIN

Once the door opens…

_____

_____

_____

_____

_____

_____

_____

_____

Though I was never diminished by…

_____

_____

_____

_____

_____

_____

_____

_____

For the longest time...

_____

_____

_____

_____

_____

_____

_____

_____

I never expected...

_____

_____

_____

_____

_____

_____

_____

_____

Sometimes I care too much about…

_____

_____

_____

_____

_____

_____

_____

_____

The next time…

_____

_____

_____

_____

_____

_____

_____

_____

I did not lose…

_____

_____

_____

_____

_____

_____

_____

_____

I never needed…

_____

_____

_____

_____

_____

_____

_____

_____

B . L Y N N G O O D W I N

Because I cannot ask you…

_____

_____

_____

_____

_____

_____

_____

_____

_____

I now know that beauty is…

_____

_____

_____

_____

_____

_____

_____

_____

_____

I've surrendered…

_____

_____

_____

_____

_____

_____

_____

_____

If I return to…

_____

_____

_____

_____

_____

_____

_____

_____

B . L Y N N G O O D W I N

Someday I hope to be...

_____
_____
_____
_____
_____
_____
_____
_____
_____

I want other caregivers to know...

_____
_____
_____
_____
_____
_____
_____
_____
_____

Spare time…

_____
_____
_____
_____
_____
_____
_____
_____

I continue to want…

_____
_____
_____
_____
_____
_____
_____
_____

B . L Y N N   G O O D W I N

I now believe…

_____

_____

_____

_____

_____

_____

_____

_____

I will always love…

_____

_____

_____

_____

_____

_____

_____

_____

I wouldn't change…

_____

_____

_____

_____

_____

_____

_____

_____

I will always be grateful that…

_____

_____

_____

_____

_____

_____

_____

_____

B. LYNN GOODWIN

Joy bubbles up when…

_____

_____

_____

_____

_____

_____

_____

_____

The life which is not examined is not worth living.

—Plato

Your Own Sentence Starts

Use these blank pages to write your own unique sentence starts. Use words, phrases, or questions.

Write about them today if you want, or save them for another time. By now, you probably have found exactly the right journal for writing outside this book.

Write as many times on one topic as you like. There's always more to say.

If the same sentence starts or prompts keep coming up, that tells you that you have more to say on the subject. Always remember, there is no wrong way to do this.

These lines will help you generate your own topics:

Today I want to write about...

I don't want to write about...

I will never write about...

Why...

When...

If...

Because...

Suggestion: List things you want to write about or don't want to write about. Write your why, when, and if questions. Journal entries can flow just as easily from questions as from sentence starts. When you run out of space, write in your journal.

If you believe in giving back to the world, share your sentence starts and questions. Send them to Writer Advice, www.writeradvice.com using the e-mail address on the website. We'll post them on the "Journaling for Caregivers" page.

You can use the same address to let me know how this book is working for you and offer suggestions for the next edition.

_____

_____

_____

_____

_____

_____

_____

_____

_____

_____

_____

_____

_____

_____

_____

_____

_____

_____

_____

_____

_____

_____

_____

_____

_____

_____

_____

_____

_____

_____

_____

_____

_____

_____

_____

_____

_____

_____

_____

_____

_____

_____

_____

_____

_____

_____

B . L Y N N G O O D W I N

Tell me what it is you plan to do with your one wild and precious life.

—Mary Oliver

Honing Your Voice

"Everyone has a story to tell about a place and a time and lessons learned," according to Carl Lennertz, author of *Cursed by a Happy Childhood: Letters from a Dad to a Daughter.* Everyone includes you.

Do you have an entry you want to develop into a letter? Have you found a universal truth you want to share with the world in a personal essay? Do you want to make yourself or your loved one into a fictitious character and explore your conflicts in a short story? Do the images of your home or the photos on a dresser lend themselves to a poem? Would you like to expand or finish a conversation in a one-act play? Do you want to combine several entries into a memoir?

What a lot of options your writing offers you. Not sure where to start?

After you've written, ask yourself two questions:

1. What do I like about my writing? Underline the words and phrases you like.
2. What do I want to know more about?

Write brief notes in the margins next to the places you want to develop. These notes will help you get started when you decide to revise and develop your writing.

If you'd like to learn more about the writing process, any of the books below will give you uplifting advice. They are available in bookstores and may be available for a three-week loan from your local library. Look them over. Read and explore. Let one book lead you to another as you carve your own writing path.

Cameron, Julia. *The Artists Way: A Spiritual Path to Higher Creativity.* Penguin Group, 2002.

Couturier, Andy. *Writing Open the Mind, Tapping the Subconscious to Free the Writing and the Writer.* Ulysses Press, 2005.

Goldberg, Natalie. *Wild Mind: Living the Writer's Life.* Bantam Books, 1990.

Lamott, Anne. *Bird by Bird: Some Instructions on Writing and Life.* Knopf Publishing Group, 1995.

Maisel, Eric, Ph.D. *Write Mind: 299 Things Writers Should Never Say to Themselves (and What They Should Say Instead).* Penguin Group, 2002.

Matson, Clive. *Let The Crazy Child Write: Finding Your Creative Writing Voice.* New World Library, 1998.

Murdock, Maureen. *Unreliable Truth: On Memoir and Memory.* Avalon Publishing Group, 2003.

Schneider, Pat, and Peter Elbow (foreword). *Writing Alone and with Others.* Oxford University Press, 2003.

Once you have drafted a story, poem, or letter you may want to share it with a writing partner or an editor before bringing it to a larger audience. You can search for editors in your community or online. If you go online, consider checking out Writer Advice, www.writeradvice.com. Writer Advice has set up a page that specializes in journaling for caregivers. Click on the "Journaling for Caregivers" button to find information about writing with other caregivers, sample prompts, writings of those who have tried the process, booklists, and more. Writer Advice also offers Manuscript Consultation Services.

Caregiving is a gift. So is writing. I hope you will share these gifts with others.

Contact Information

Contact author B. Lynn Goodwin through her website, www.writeradvice.com or e-mail her at Lgood67334@comcast.net.

Learn the latest news about upcoming workshops and appearances, submissions opportunities, and more by clicking on the "Journaling for Caregivers" button on Writer Advice, www.writeradvice.com.

Author B. Lynn Goodwin is a freelance writer,  former caregiver, and retired drama and English teacher who worked in both high school and college. Her writing has been published in numerous newspapers, magazines, anthologies, and e-zines. In addition to teaching workshops on caregiving and writing for other publications, Lynn writes reviews and author interviews for *Writer Advice,* www.writeradvice.com and is the founder and managing editor of the e-zine, which celebrated its ten-year anniversary in October of 2007.